Soul Ties
&
Legal Ground

by
Jessica Jones and Susan Samuels

Soul Ties & Legal Ground

By Jessica Jones and Susan Samuels

Published by
> Quiddity Press & Productions
> Suite 3102, 115 Tidecrest Pkwy., Ponte Vedra, FL 32081 U.S.A.

Any resemblance of names or places to actual events or locales, any persons, living or dead, is entirely coincidental.

First Printing 2009.
Printed in the United States of America

Quiddity Press & Productions
Suite 3102, 115 Tidecrest Pkwy.,
Ponte Vedra, FL 32081 U.S.A.

Publisher's Cataloging-In-Publication
(Provided by Quiddity Press & Publications)

Jones, Jessica; Samuels, Susan. – 1st ed.

LCCN:
ISBN-13: 978-0-9814548-3-2
ISBN-10: 0-9814548-3-6

Table of Contents

Introduction

Few people have seen "Soul Ties". Few people really understand the mechanics and science behind "Soul Ties". But this has not stopped numerous people from stepping forward as experts on the subject. And the information has been both erroneous and plagued with the processes of man's logic instead of God's truth. Thus, as a result, further misleading those very sheep who most need to understand the truth.

I was given the office of Seer Prophet before my birth. Unfortunately, with that office, I was not given an owner's manual and so had to learn the tenants of the office through trial and error. Most Christian circles would call that a "mixture", which has led me down the path of learning how to recognize and cast out the mixture, while keeping the pure stream of God. However, through the process, I learned the tenants of both worlds: God's world and Satan's world, the knowledge of which I use to forward God's truth and tenants.

The first four years of my life I lived in vision. Isolated from human contact, I spent my days and nights among the angels. I was virtually brought up by angels, entertained by angels. The next twenty-one years I found myself thrown into the world of Lucifer and his much less pleasant, fallen angels. I learned the dogma of their religion and ways. The following two decades was a time wrought with the struggle of getting out of that demonic kingdom back to God's side, again with very little understanding or assistance from others. The last twelve years I have been fully sold out to God, kicking Lucifer's butt everywhere I find his deceitful hand on the lives of God's people.

I have been led through a most interesting career in the supernatural realm from the aspects of all three heavens. What this memorable, and not necessarily enviable, career has afforded me is a unique perspective in the workings of the demonic and a deep understanding of how the enemy works.

I have not only seen "Soul Ties" but I have used them, used the control they afforded me. And because I have used them, I understand them in ways others have not grasped or considered.

So this book is dedicated to revealing the workings of "Soul Ties" so that God's people can finally free themselves from the bondage and power of these insidious "Ties". My desire is to break their power in every life, freeing God's people into a deeper level of liberty, life and truth.

I can say definitively, without question, that there are NO such things as "GODLY SOUL-TIES"!

In fact, there are not even "Soul Ties" taught in the Bible. This is, instead, a New Age theology that has pervaded Christian circles. Christians teaching about "Soul Ties" have never seen a "Soul Tie" and consequently are espousing things they have been taught by someone else who likewise has never seen a "Soul Tie".

The word *soul* comes from the Hebrew word *nephesh* which simply means **a *breathing creature; the breathing substance of being; the inner being of man; the seat of appetites; emotions and passions; the activity of the character.***

The Greek word for *soul* is *psuche* which means exactly the same thing — *the breath of life; the vital force which animates a body; the seat of feelings, desires, affections and aversions; the soul regarded as a mortal being designed for everlasting life; the soul as an essence which differs from the body and is not dissolved by death.*

Neither one of these definitions lends itself to giving the soul the ability to create a "Tie" or "bond" of any style. The soul cannot in and of itself tie or join itself to someone or something else. It is simply not designed to do this. These "Ties" are a spiritual matter.

What does the Bible say about "Soul Ties"?

The Bible says absolutely nothing about "Soul Ties". The idea of "Soul Ties" is a man-made speculation onto which some teachers overlay scripture in an attempt to explain certain human behaviors.

The Bible does speak of close friendships, such as that of David and Jonathan. This is simply a way of expressing Jonathan's total commitment to, and deep friendship with, David. The attempt to twist this passage into a mystical binding of the actual soul is unwarranted.

> *The soul of Jonathan was knit (tied together mentally in love) with the soul of David, and Jonathan loved him as his own soul. (1 Samuel 18:1 NKJV)*

> *By the time David had finished speaking to Sha'ul, Y'honatan found himself inwardly drawn by David's character, so that Y'honatan loved him as he did himself...Y'honatan made a covenant with David, because he loved him as he did himself. (1 Samuel 18:1, 3 TCJB)*

Using the New King James Version we can see how modern Christians can become confused if they have not done a word study of the word *knit*. However, the Complete Jewish Bible explains, from the original Hebrew, a more accurate picture of what actually transpired between these two friends. They made a covenant of love and friendship with each other according to the laws Jesus set out in Matthew 22:37-40. They were following the Lord's commandments in a way few people today allow such a law to be fulfilled.

There are Godly friendships. In fact, we are to nurture Godly relationships that consist of loyalty, love and great depth of compassion. However, as we can see in the friendship between David and Jonathon, Jonathon did not allow his feelings and loyalties to interfere with his daily obligations and duties. And neither did he let his daily duties to the king interfere with or harm David.

It is a loss to mankind, and a loss to the friendships we are supposed to nurture, that these relationships have been encased in innuendo and sexual overtones. The unclean spirits of lust have had great success in not only destroying what

God has commanded but also in creating a terrible, crippling fear of relationships and friendships. We have stepped away from a Godly love to a humanistic and animal lust. And if no sexual overtones exist between two friends, then gossip quickly develops one in destructive accusation.

We have lost and broken the commandments of God through our lusts and fears.

If two men, or two women especially if one is married, develop friendships, immediately it dissolves into the realm of gossip, innuendo, distrust and offence. We have successfully built walls around what we deem acceptable. The office of Satan and his large number of minions of fallen angels have effectively precluded that we cannot fulfill the commandments of Christ for fear of falling into disrepute with our peers.

Although there is no example of a Godly "Soul Tie" in the Bible, because they do not exist, there are dozens of examples of real "Soul Ties" and their eventual and disappointing outcome. Although I will be going into greater detail in later chapters to show why these are "Soul Ties", let me give a few examples here.

- Saul and David (2 Samuel 22)
- Solomon and his wives/concubines (1 Kings 11)
- Adam and Eve (Genesis 3)
- Ahab and Jezebel (1 Kings 18)
- Job and his children (Job)
- David and Absalom (1 Chronicles 3)
- Amnon and Tamar (2 Samuel 13)

- Ananias and Sapphira (Acts 5)
- Saul and Samuel (1 Samuel 28)
- Corinthian church (1 Corinthians)

Every example of "Soul Ties" in the Bible comes with a disastrous ending which is a warning to cleanse ourselves of their hold and effects at every opportunity.

There are a myriad of different types of "Soul Ties". Each one is created through a strong emotional experience. Different types of "Soul Ties" between two people are:

- Fortune Teller and client
- Parent and Child
  - o Mother/Father and Child
  - o Mother/Father and Dead Child
- Friends
- Stalker and victim
- Rapist/Assaulter and victim
- Student and Teacher
- Sexual partners
- Person and object
- Person and pet
- Person and familiar spirit
- Mass hysteria group
- Generational "Soul Ties"
- Inquisition "Soul Ties"
- Terror "Soul Ties"
- Survivor "Soul Ties"
- Stockholm syndrome "Soul Ties"
- Generational vows, promises, dedications, curses

There are many different types of "Soul Ties" but the way to get rid of them is fortunately very simple and easy.

Chapter 1:
The Mechanics of "Soul Ties"

In the previous chapter we examined the meaning of the word *soul*. The concept that the soul, which is the sum of our experiences making up our personality and memories, is spiritually powerful enough to reach out and bind itself to someone else borders on science fiction rather than logic. In fact, it gives a power to people long dreamed of but not God-given. Our power and authority comes through Jesus alone, through the power of His sacrifice and blood. Our greatest *power* rests in the power of our words, that power coming from the authority given us through Jesus Christ. We do not have the authority to reach out and create a spiritual bond with someone else just because we feel like it. This is a mystical teaching which lends power to witches and warlocks, druids and mystics.

As mentioned previously, there is no mention of "Soul Ties" in the Bible. There must be a reason God does not mention them, could it be that they are not of His creation? He mentions dietary laws, dress codes, sexual practices, religious practices, ceremonial requirements, relationships, hair requirements, ear piercing...because these are all things He has created and does not want perverted. But He is totally silent on "Soul Ties". If they were His creation, He would have expressed the difference between those created by Him and those created by the enemy, including instruction on what to do when we become the victim of the latter.

But He has said nothing.

Colossians 2:2 tells us about hearts being knit together in love, just like Jonathan's and David's hearts were knit together in love. This is the love that Jesus talked about in His commandments — that we love each other as we love ourselves. It does not speak of "Soul Ties". That speculation is stretching our imagination at its best to try and make the scriptures fit into current theology.

Do not confuse "heart love" with "Soul Ties".

God is silent about "Soul Ties". Why?

The soul consists of our mind, emotions and will. When we die, the spirit returns to God (Ecclesiastes 12:7), the soul goes to judgment (Ecclesiastes 12:7), and the body returns to the earth (Genesis 3:19). The experiences of the soul, the essence of who we are, begin the moment we are created. Many believe that we are with God before we are born. Many remember being with God before they were born which seems to prove that we had life before coming to this natural realm where we now find ourselves. What form of life, we can only speculate. But the Lord has told several people, Jeremiah for one, that He knew them before they were born (Jeremiah 1:5).

"Soul Ties" are created from strong emotion. The mechanics are simple. The soul creates a strong emotion which triggers a spirit (fallen angel/demon) within that person to create a "spiritual tie" with another person, animal or thing. This "spiritual tie" looks like a smooth flexible straw and works very much like a super highway or conduit through

15

which spirits locate and travel from one person to another. Each end of the straw is connected to the persons, animal or thing involved. If there is no person or animal on the other end, the "spiritual tie" is connected to a spirit represented by the object, or even dead person/animal.

The mechanics are uncomplicated. "Soul Ties" are triggered by emotion, are created by spirits, are spiritual in nature, and can only be broken or removed through prayer and spiritual warfare.

Each "Soul Tie" is a different color, allowing an experienced *user* to follow a specific "Soul Tie" to a particular person. I have used this technique throughout my years (past tense) to find people who I had lost touch with. It is a very effective tool to use and is freely used by spirits to go to their assigned destinations quickly without hindrance.

To view the world through spiritual eyes that can see into that realm is like seeing the largest, most intricate nest of insidious but very colorful spiders' webs. People have thousands of these "Ties" connected to them at any one time unless they have been diligently removed. Considering they accumulate over time and only decrease with prayer and spiritual warfare, people become weighed down with these attachments throughout their life.

Below is a very simple representation of what they look like. Multiply it by hundreds and in some cases thousands and you have a closer representation of how they work.

It has taken me years of prayer and vigilance to break off these "Soul Ties" that not only I created but others created with me. The very first "deliverance" experience I had with breaking off these "Soul Ties" took me totally by surprise. A pastor, who had no understanding of the impact of what he was doing, broke off the "Soul Ties" from a friend. I was sitting in the same room when I felt a sudden overwhelming tsunami wave of spirits. I crumpled under the impact of their onslaught. As the "Ties" were broken, every spirit that had been connected with those "Soul Ties" came flooding back onto me. It was a singularly terrifying moment.

This is to emphasize that where one "Soul Tie" is created, usually scores and hundreds of "Ties" are created. Rarely is a person the victim of only one "Tie". And with each "Tie" anywhere from one to a thousand or more spirits have taken residence as they use these "Ties" as *superhighways* to travel through the natural and spiritual realm of this dimension.

Another serious experience I had concerned the "Soul Ties" I had with my cherished poodle. Without realizing the consequence of what I was doing, I broke off all the "Soul Ties" out of obedience to be faithful to the Lord. However, the people who taught about "Soul Ties" neglected to mention that both ends of the "Soul Tie" needed to be broken so that the spirits did not boomerang back onto the person or animal who still maintained a connection. Without breaking the "Soul Tie" properly, I condemned my dog to the full brunt of spirits of fear. He lost ten pounds in one week and died almost immediately of a devastating disease. This may have been overlooked had this particular disease not been caused specifically by the spirit of fear.

I have learned my lessons the hard way at great cost. Those who treat "Soul Ties" lightly or teach that there are Godly "Soul Ties" are doing God's people an injustice. It is serious business indeed and not one to be taken flippantly or without a proper understanding. This is not to suggest that you should be afraid of them. It is to say that you should become aware of how they work, and the very simple way to remove them.

When you understand how they actually work, a simple prayer will rid you of the effects with no cost or backlash. The objective of this book is to make this process as easy as possible for you so you too can experience the freedom and liberty of a life that is yours alone without any unhealthy attachments.

Chapter 2:
Generational "Soul Ties"

Generational "Soul Ties" are the bonds that have grown from generation to generation and pass from parent to child. They are created by words of dedication, curses and vows, through the bond of parent and child, sexual molestation, lack of nurturing, any emotional open door, demands of performance, etc.

Generational "Soul Ties" looks much like a very large well, narrow at the originating ancestors, becoming increasingly wider towards the present. The walls of the well are constructed not of stone, but of a flexible straw system resembling twisted, aged roots. They wrap and twist around creating a yawning trap waiting for an unaware victim. With the proper vision, you can follow these roots to their source, thus discovering the root or cause of a particular problem.

Following these root systems to their origins is very much how I am able to delve into the generational past of a person and know what is required to free them from the particular incident in their generations. These root systems are very complex and shrouded in an ancient, antique aspect that is uncomfortable and almost eerie.

These generational "Ties" bind us to the traits and curses of our ancestors. Underlying these curses always lay the inheritances that God has put into our family line which can be seen as soon as the debris and underbrush is taken away.

It is difficult to accurately show what it is that I see when I look into the world of "Soul Ties", but a section of the wall would look very much like the below picture. Although not completely accurate, it is the closest representation that I could find.

Each root or tube connects from one moment in one ancestor's life into the web of our generational bloodline. It carries with it the generational spirits that were active in their life. These spirits become active in our lives because of the legal ground through our ancestry.

Our siblings inherit the same root system although there will be different curses or active lines and spirits that will manifest. This is because there are different inheritances and underlying gifts at work.

There is a reason that so few of us know who our ancestors were. I know my maternal ancestors only back to great-grandfather. My father's side is even less. I know only as far back as my grandmother. There is little information except the general nationalities that make up my bloodline. I know that I am a mix of all the UK countries and German. But in order to be free of the generational "Ties" that plague my life, I need to know more detail.

At one time, everyone knew their ancestry. It was unusual to not live in the same location forever. It has only been in recent centuries that this has changed. People began to travel and emigrate partly in an effort to forget, or separate from their pasts and create new lives. As the Kingdom of God becomes more focused, and we want to be free of the problems and curses to pick up our inheritances put in the line by God, we find ourselves unable to identify our linage.

But we can generalize our family past. For example, I can take what I know as my general bloodline and research a history of the people. From that research, I can do a blanket deliverance to make sure all my bases are covered.

For example, I know that my last name, Jones, is Welsh. However, my father was Irish. I learned from the history of the Irish that they scoured the coastline of England and Scotland and stole children to take back to Ireland for slaves. Add to this the fact that my father was sold by his mother to a farmer when he was nine years old, I can assume quite accurately that I come from a line of slaves. It does not take much imagination to realize the horror and fear in the lives of those children under their Irish taskmasters. I can work on these general issues and free myself from that part of the generational "Soul Tie" wall surrounding my life.

Another example is the German heritage from my grandmother's side. Although I know her family were farmers here in Canada, Germans were conquerors and settlers of the entire European world. They seeded every country in Europe at one time or another. In fact, Germans sat on the English throne and many words in English have German origins such as Kindergarten, hinterland, pretzel, blitz, poltergeist, rucksack, etc.

Now I can look at the German general history, knowing that my ancestors were conquerors, yes, but they were farmers who ran before the onslaught of the Huns and Romans to faraway lands. My grandmother was an entrepreneur and had a keen business mind. So I assume that her family was part of the group that fled from the Huns. They were townspeople, most likely shop owners of some sort.

I can deduce a great degree of fear from both sides of the family. My grandfather was Scottish. He was actually the illegitimate son of a Scottish barmaid. She sold him to Scottish immigrants who were going to start a new life in Canada. He was never adopted by his new family although he was treated like a son. Knowing this brief history, after researching the history of Edinborough and how the city was created, I know the horror the poor barmaid lived in during her life. I know through an educated guess how and where she lived and the conditions that beset her, forcing her to give up her son. I can deal with that history because I have done my homework.

Every knee shall bow and since I am the only relative of my line that is Christian and following the heart of God, then it is my responsibility to stand up for my family line and say,

"The buck stops here. I take responsibility for the things my family has done." It costs me nothing except the realization that my family was not the wonderful people I would have preferred. Instead, they were human just like everyone else. They were human like me. It costs me nothing to stand before God and repent of some aspect, every aspect that could possibly have been done in my family line, and place it below the feet of Jesus. Every sin in my family line will be laid beneath the feet of Jesus, becoming His footstool.

> *Exodus 20:5; Deuteronomy 5:9 I the Lord thy God am a jealous God, visiting the iniquity of the fathers upon the children unto the third and fourth generation.*

I do not want those sins in my life. I want them under the feet of Jesus. I need to look into the history of my generational lines to free myself from that sin. I need to free myself from the curses, vows, dedications, words and sins, and it will take some research and prayerful consideration.

Every knee shall bow and since I am the representative for my family line, then I shall bow my knee in their name. Standing in their stead will redeem my family line in the name of Jesus. We inherit not only the family inheritances but the curses from both lines that come through mother and father...not just father alone as some have suggested. Jesus was declared through both genealogies of mother and father in the New Testament because we inherit both family lines and histories.

If, as some suggested, we only inherit from our father, then our DNA would only be from our father instead of made up of both parents. If science and scripture recognize both lines, how is it that some preachers only teach the father's generational line leaving people only half-free?

I encourage you to research your possible roots and pray the following over everything you find.

ぬるぬ

Father God, I praise You and thank You for Your mercy and love. Father, You have extended to me Your mercy. You have preserved my family line so that I would be born. I praise You and thank You for that. And Lord, I now bow my knee as the representative of my family line. I bow my knee for every ancestor in my line that did not know You or understand Your protective care in their lives. I bow my knee and say, "The Lord my God, the Lord is one. There is no other god before You." Lord, I break the power of every "Soul Tie" that came through my family line, on both my father and mother's side, all the way back to Adam and Eve. Father, I repent that I have allowed these "Soul Ties" to work in my life; I renounce and fall out of agreement with them. Father, I break their power in my life, and every spirit that came through those "Ties", I break their power and cancel their assignment in my life. And Lord, for (insert any specific concern or knowledge) I now repent, renounce and fall out of agreement with the "Soul Tie" of (example: Druidism) that came through (example: my mother's line); I repent, renounce and fall out of agreement that I allowed this "Tie" to work in my life and I break the power and cancel the assignment of the (example: Druidism) all the way back to Adam and Eve; I break the power and cancel the assignment of every spirit of (example: witchcraft, old ways, traditions and ceremonies) that came through those "Soul Ties" and I send it to the pit reserved for demons that will bind them for one thousand years, in the name of Jesus. I apply the blood of Jesus over every wound and attachment and Lord, I ask for healing and deliverance. Father, I place this sin under the feet of Jesus and claim the inheritance that you entrusted to my family line and activate it in my life now, in the name of Jesus. Amen.

Chapter 3:
Emotional "Soul Ties"

Emotional "Soul Ties" are difficult to control until one learns how to control their emotions. Any strong emotion such as hate, fear, love, bitterness, grief, anger, vengeance, etc. all trigger the creation of "Soul Ties".

From this point on, I will call "Soul Ties" by their more appropriate name of "Spirit Ties" because they are spiritual in nature, not of the natural realm.

The soul feels the intensity of the emotion but it is the spirit within that creates the tie. In order to get rid of these types of spirit ties one must deal with the issue of the emotion and the reason for the issue.

Following is a very basic example most people have felt on some level. This actually happened to a friend of mine. She was driving the speed limit in her car, which apparently made the driver behind her extremely irate. When she stopped at a red light, the driver in the car behind got out of his car and accosted her verbally through her now closed window. He actually spit upon her window before returning to his vehicle, continuing his loud verbal abuse all the way.

She was shaken by the sudden confrontation. She couldn't shake it through the normal avenues of deliverance. We tried breaking the trauma and still she was shaken. It was not until we broke the spirit tie the driver had created with her was she released from the trauma of the situation. The spirit of bitterness, anger and intimidation had created a spirit tie with her triggered by the extreme emotion of irrational hatred the other driver exhibited towards her. Perhaps he had carried that anger for days as she was visibly shaken for days. Once the spirit tie was broken, the spirits that had transferred because of the tie were cast out and peace returned to her.

This is a very simple example to show you just how quickly and easily these ties are created. For the few seconds it takes to create one, it is broken and removed just as quickly and easily.

To reiterate the mechanics, the person feels the emotion in their soul, a spirit within the person takes the opportunity of that trauma and strong emotion to create a spiritual bond/tie with another person/animal/thing/ spirit, and then spirits will travel back and forth through the tube-like spirit tie. To break it, one simply needs to pray, breaking the tie at both ends and casting it along with any spirit that has used it or remains in it into the pit in the name of Jesus.

There is nothing complicated about this but there is something extremely liberating about the process. You can finally be freed from life-long bonds and ties in a way you have never imagined.

Another example of an emotional tie is the story of a mother whose first pregnancy brought forth a still-born child. Her nine months of expectation ended with devastation. At the traumatic news that her child was dead, the spirit of grief entered. Her grief was inconsolable. The spirit of grief had taken the opportunity to create a spirit tie to the dead child. Since the body returns to dust, the spirit tie was actually created with a well of grief spirits represented by the body of the child. The woman could not bond with the three daughters she had later. She could never shake the grief of her missing daughter. She had counseling and deliverance, but it was not until the spirit tie was broken that she found relief. Her relationship with her other children improved remarkably as she was finally free from the hounding grief.

We see an example of this in 2 Samuel 22 where Saul hated David so much that a spirit tie was created between Saul and David. How do we know this? Saul became obsessed with David. He could not get David out of his mind or his heart for one moment. He hunted David for years with unrelenting determination. The more his hatred seethed, the more spirit ties were created and the more Saul opened himself up to spirits of insanity. He finished off his illustrious career in 1 Samuel 28 when he created a spirit tie with both the witch of Endor and the spirit she conjured up to represent Samuel.

Another example is between Job and his children. Job was a righteous man until he became fearful for the souls of his children. His children did not live the pious life of Job. They partied. And after every party, Job would do the customary sacrifices on their behalf lest they sinned during the party. Job was terrified they would not go to be with the Lord but that they would sin and go to hell. This caused the Lord to step in and hand Job over to Lucifer for a season to bring to light Job's fear, causing Job to acknowledge his own circumstance.

We see another instance in 1 Chronicles 3 between David and Absalom. David had an over-the-top love for his son that blinded him to all Absalom did. The abnormal level of love David felt caused spirit ties to be created between the two. David's blind love increased and Absalom began to detest his father so much that he conspired to kill him and take the throne.

2 Samuel 11 tells us the story of David and Bathsheba where David's lust of the eyes grew to such a level that David not only was willing to break the laws of God and commit adultery, but he was also willing to order the murder of Bathsheba's husband.

David had a problem with spirit ties because he was a passionate man. He lived loudly and loved loudly. The problem continued on with his children. Amnon and Tamar of 2 Samuel 13 had the same problem as their father. Amnon had an abnormal love for his sister which created a spirit tie between them. Amnon became so obsessed with his sister that he raped her under the delusion that she loved him as well.

Acts 5 tells us of the story of Ananias and Sapphira who were so obsessed with their money, which was theirs to do with as they wished, that they lied to the Holy Spirit by giving only a portion of their money, claiming it was all. They had a spirit tie with the spirit of Mammon. And for their lie, they died on the spot before the apostle.

The Bible is rife with examples of spirit ties if one cares to look for them, and every one of them ends badly for the person who is bound by them. It proves once again that there are no such things as Godly "Soul Ties".

Where did spirit ties come from?

As the people of God we are to have the Holy Spirit within us. That Holy Spirit is to witness between two people. But Lucifer did not have that. There was no witness with anything he did after he began to fall. So he, who knew the workings of the spiritual realm completely, began to create and experiment with spirit ties.

When a spirit tie is created between two people, it is an open highway for spirits to travel back and forth between the two people. It is an open invitation for like spirits to enter in as well.

Have you ever wondered why you suddenly become angry for no reason? Or hostile, depressed, anxious, frightened, etc? Look around you to the people you know and find out who has an issue of anger, hostility, depression, anxiousness, fear, etc. You have a spirit tie with that person and their spirits are affecting you.

The solution? Thankfully it is very simple. Just pray the following prayer as often as needed and you will be free of all your spirit ties.

Take note that you may have more than one spirit tie and so you will have to pray for each one as often as they arise. And new ones may have been created. I personally am the target of a spirit tie created by another person regularly. The tell-tale sign is irritable bowel syndrome. It takes me a minute or three to figure it out, but as soon as I break the spirit tie and cast out the spirits of fear, stress, anxiety, colitis, hatred, vengeance, jealousy and irritable bowel syndrome, the symptoms immediately disappear and everything is back to normal. It happens so instantaneously, it is amazing. Just cover the bases of what you see operating in the other person.

This prayer works. I use it all the time and have remained spirit tie free for several years now.

෴

Father God, I repent, renounce and fall out of agreement with the spirit tie that I have allowed to be created. Father, I break this spirit tie off and I break its power and cancel its assignment in my life. I break the power and cancel the assignment of every spirit of fear, stress, anxiety, (and name any others you may be aware of here), in my life. In the name of Jesus I command now that every spirit named be cast into the pit. Holy Spirit, I ask you to restore me to peace and health, and I command now in the name of Jesus that every cell, tissue, bone, etc. come back into complete alignment with how God created me. I speak peace to my body, soul and spirit, in the name of Jesus.

This is Satan's most widely used and most veiled tool. He has successfully kept peopled bound and unproductive, not to mention sick and dying. The good news is that once exposed it is both readily recognizable and easily broken. Trust the Holy Spirit to bring it to your attention, and the authority you have in the name of Jesus Christ to break the hold in your life.

Chapter 4:
Sexual "Soul Ties"

The two primary methods used to create spirit ties are through a very strong emotional bond, already discussed, and through bodily fluids transferred through the sexual act. Sounds like an STD? This is not a co-incidence.

A spirit tie is always created through a sexual act. The natural body is vulnerable, giving the same opportunity to spirits as does a trauma. Emotions are always heightened through sexual intercourse regardless of the circumstances.

> *Or do you not know that he who is joined to a harlot is one body with her? For "the two," He says, "shall become one flesh. (1 Corinthians 6:16 NKJV)*

To join is from Hebrew word *lavah* meaning *to twine, to unite, to remain*; also **to borrow as a form of obligation** or *to lend; to join oneself to, to be joined unto,* **to cause to borrow,** *to lend to.*

It does speak about cleaving one to another.

The word *cleave* comes from the Hebrew word *chazaq* which means **to fasten upon, to seize, to bind, restrain, conquer,** *to make severe, to hold, to contain, to strengthen oneself,* **to hold strongly with.**

We are joined one with another through every and any sexual encounter. A spirit tie is created and has to be removed. This is another area where the church says there are Godly "Soul Ties" because sex is a God-given gift. However, we are to be one in body, in love, in Christ...there is nothing in scripture that says we are to be one in "Soul Tie". And if the scriptures are silent on this matter, when so much is said about every other matter, it must be because it is not of God.

This union is a natural process which is a precept and commandment of God. But added to this natural process are the spirits. Now let's break down the process as it happens the way God planned it and how the spirits have changed it.

God planned that sexual intercourse would be a natural extension of love; wholesome, righteous, pure love without the complications of spirits. Let's examine this for a minute.

A man and a woman are to love each other with a Godly love. It is a deeper level of Godly love than two friends might experience because the husband and wife are one flesh. This is the precept of God. It was designed so that there would be no conflict or hurt inflicted because a person's natural instinct is to *NOT* hurt one's own flesh. There is a deeper level of understanding of God's love here because we are an extension of Him, one flesh so to speak.

This is shown in several examples in the Bible. We are called the "sons of God" (Luke 20:36). We are called "the body of Christ" (Romans 12:5). We are called "the Bride of Christ" (2 Corinthians 11:2; Isaiah 54:5). We are called "the children of God" (1 John 3:2). We are called "joint heirs with Christ" (Romans 8:17).

We are to experience all these levels of God's love in our life, but the closest relationship is husband and wife. We become one flesh.

And on this level we are to realize that God would never hurt His own flesh. He supplies every need for His Bride, His love, His flesh because He knows what we need before we do — because we are one. And He would never do anything or allow us anything that would harm us because He would never harm Himself. He wants only the best for us as He wants only the best for Himself.

The commandments of God are not just empty words or difficult laws. They are laws He lives by Himself. He loves Himself and because He loves Himself, He can love us the same way and to the same depth. "Greater love has no one than this, than to lay down one's life for his friends." (John 15:13 NKJ). Jesus loved God over His own life. Jesus loved us, His Bride, over His own life. He fulfilled the commandments of the law totally and completely while we were and are still struggling with the idea/concepts of love, generosity, unforgiveness, etc.

On the ten-step ladder to righteousness found in the Ten Commandments (Exodus 20:2-17; Deuteronomy 5:6-21) we seem to still be struggling with loving God. On the simpler three-step commandments given by Jesus (Matthew 22:37-40), we are still struggling with loving ourselves.

We cannot love God or anyone else until we accept and love ourselves. And we cannot fully love ourselves until we divest ourselves of all the lies Lucifer and his "support staff" have told us, and we start believing the truth. We were created especially, singularly because God loves exactly who we are. To not love ourselves just as we are is to call God, our Creator, Lover, Husband, Brother, Father, and Friend a liar. And I personally do not want to ever tread in that water.

If this is what marriage is to be, then why is there so much work to make a successful marriage? It is such hard work because we enter into marriage loving the other person on some level but with an incredibly high mixture of self, selfishness and self-will. We invariably get in the way of that marriage just as much as we get in the way of our marriage with God.

Selah!

Alright, becoming one flesh is a natural process. The concept is a principle and therefore applies not only within marriage, unfortunately. We become one flesh with every sexual partner. This includes high-school sweethearts, friends, lovers, prostitutes/customers, rapist/victim, molester/victim, casual acquaintances, and people/animals who participate in bestiality.

Sexual spirit ties open the way to being sidetracked in our walk with God. Look at the story of Solomon and his seven hundred wives and three hundred concubines (1 Kings). Solomon turned from following the Lord to building the high places that were repugnant to the Lord.

Another example is in Genesis 3, the story of Adam and Eve. Adam was so blinded by his spirit tie with his wife Eve that when she sinned, he did not step forward as a righteous husband to restore her to the Lord, instead he was terrified of losing her so sinned right alongside her. His spirit tie caused him to throw away eternity with his Lord as well as the future of all his children.

Ahab was also blinded by his spirit tie with Jezebel, letting her commit murder for him. His blind loyalty to his heathen wife allowed her to commit genocide of the prophets of God to raise up her false prophets in their stead. He threw away his God as he helplessly stood by, ushering in her god to the people.

And finally we have the Corinthian church. What began as a little indiscretion between two people (as if it could actually be called an indiscretion) spread through the Corinthian church unchecked. They were rife with sexual spirit ties which had to be addressed by Paul.

The insidious reality about sexual spirit ties is that you are not only tied to your current sexual partner but you have a tie with everyone they slept with and everyone they slept with and everyone they slept with…lets call it a downline.

Each time you have sexual intercourse with someone, you give them a piece of your heart. If this is a casual incident, you end up with a splintered heart that has pieces scattered around the world. Your heart is no longer whole. And you end up with a piece of the other person's heart in you. You end up shattered and splintered unless it is within marriage and you are as one flesh. The term brokenhearted takes on new meaning.

You can see the safety of being faithful in your marriage, but now you can also see the importance of keeping yourself clean spiritually as well.

Victims of molestation or rape, end up with a piece of their attacker, and they have taken a piece of the victim with them. Add to this, the fact that the victim is now bound to that person spiritually as well as naturally. Add to this, there is now free access to their spirits. A person who is raped will have a plethora of otherwise unexplained spirits, which torment and torture them long after the incident is over.

If you are a rape or molestation victim you have not only the spirits of grief, bitterness, hatred, fear, stress, anxiety, shame, unclean, etc., but rage, victim/attacker, lust, etc. These ties and spirits need to be removed before the healing can begin. Only then, will the healing take place miraculously quickly.

ഗ൙ൟ

Father God, I repent, renounce and fall out of agreement with all the spirit ties I have allowed to be created with me or that I have created. Father, I repent for having sexual intercourse with (name all the names you remember, envision the people you cannot remember). I repent of all the spirit ties I allowed to be created each time we had sexual intercourse. Father God, I break those spirit ties now in the name of Jesus. I break them off on both sides and every spirit of fear, stress and anxiety as well as every spirit of (Be inventive here. If you have gained any emotional symptom that is not naturally you (such as anger, distrust, sudden fear, promiscuousness, etc.) I bind you now in the name of Jesus. I break your power and cancel your assignment in my life in the name of Jesus. I command you now, in the name of Jesus, go to the pit where you will be held for one thousand years. Holy Spirit, I ask you to retrieve every shard of my heart and return it to me. I ask you to make my heart whole. I ask that you pour the balm of Gilead into my heart and heal it from the inside out. Father God, I ask that you heal me completely and wholly. Holy Spirit, I ask that you take back every piece of heart that I have that does not belong to me and return it to its rightful owner. Lord God Almighty, I want nothing that is not mine. Restore me as You created me to be. Lord God, I forgive everyone who has molested me, raped me or who has sex with me (this not include your spouse unless you were forced to have sexual intercourse without your full consent) and I forgive myself for what I have allowed myself to participate in. Lord God Almighty, I forgive You for not rescuing me from that situation when I so cried out for You to help me. Lord, hold nothing against them on my account, but I release them now, in the name of Jesus. Lord, I apply the blood of Jesus to every cell of my body that has been violated and I ask for Your healing mercy. I now lay my life under Your feet. Wash away my sins from Your and my memory. Take away the ping from my heart and my mind. Forgive me Lord for the sins I have committed against You, others and myself, in the name of Jesus.

Chapter 5:
Stalking "Soul Ties"

Stalking spirit ties may seems like a silly notion and not relevant to most people. But I believe that on some level a lot of people, especially in recent times, are subject to this problem.

This spirit responds to any unnatural tendency to obsess even slightly over another person, pet or thing. Perhaps a better title would be "Obsessive Soul Ties" because that is exactly what triggers this spirit tie.

And the level of obsession can be anything digressing from normal interest.

But of course, what is normal. Normal is what God considers normal. In all things respect the other one's choice and will. Respect their boundaries at all times. Honor them. Prefer them.

This is what God does regardless of how much it hurts him to be rejected by any of us. He does not take on the spirit of rejection because He is firm and accepting of Himself. But He does leave us to make choices, waiting for the moment, that one singular moment that we reach out to Him even for the briefest time. He may long for relationship with us, but He will not push the situation. He respects the free will He gave us, that very same free will that often rejects the God who created us.

But stalking spirit ties are insidious in their destruction mainly of the stalker. Through those ties flood spirits of rejection which fuel even greater responses of obsession.

In today's society there seems to be an increasing need to fill the loneliness and isolation people feel. Society is filled not only with stalkers, but internet stalkers — they can come right into your homes. They steal our identities; they steal our children and prey upon our vulnerability. Our emails are filled with scams that stalk us mercilessly; we are being hedged in everywhere we turn.

We are surrounded with stalking spirit ties as society becomes more evil and more desperate to find security at someone else's expense. This includes school cliques who have a desperate need to be the elite clique of choice. This includes gang members recruiting new members to fill their ranks.

We are surrounded by stalker spirit ties even though we have been unable to rightfully identify the problem. It is time to rethink situations and properly identify the root of the problem — many times this is stalking spirit ties.

I will include two prayers in this section. One prayer for yourself and one prayer for family members or friends you would like to be freed from these spiritual ties.

Individual prayer:

Father God, I repent, renounce and fall out of agreement with every stalking spirit tie that I have allowed to be created with me or that I have created with others. Father, I am so sorry that I wanted to be so accepted by others that I have placed myself in the situation of either being stalked by (name names) or stalking (name names). Father God, forgive me as I forgive (name names) and myself. Father God, I command that every spirit that came in through that spirit tie that their power is broken and their assignment is cancelled in my life. I command them now, in the name of Jesus, to go to the pit where they belong. Holy Spirit, I ask that you heal me. Give to me a revelation of how accepted I am by God, my Father. Give me a revelation of how accepted I am by Jesus, His Son. Give to me a revelation of how accepted I am by You, my Comforter. Heal my heart and mind and body. In Jesus' name, amen.

Family member or friend prayer.

Father God, I bind every stalking spirit tie that (name names) has allowed to be created with them (him or her) or that they have created with others. Father, I bind the power of every spirit that came through that spirit tie until (name names) has the opportunity to repent themselves and get delivered. Show them (him/her) that she/he is accepted by You. Father God, give them a revelation of Your love for them. Holy Spirit, heal him/her. Give to him/her a revelation of how accepted he/she is by God, my Father. Give him/her a revelation of how accepted he/she is by Jesus, His Son. Give to him/her a revelation of how accepted she/he is by You, their Comforter. Heal their heart and mind and body. In Jesus' name, amen.

Chapter 6:
Vows, Promises, Curses, Dedications and Verbal "Soul Ties"

One of the most disastrous weapons Lucifer has the ability to use against us is the power of our very own words. We curse ourselves almost daily. We seem to believe it is alright to call ourselves "stupid", "clumsy", etc. We believe this, or worse, we do not even think about our words, because of the lies we have come to embrace into our lives. These lies did not originate from anyone else but the enemy of our souls, Lucifer.

For me, this has been one of the hardest things to stop — cursing myself. The other thing that I need to watch is making senseless vows without thinking. Things like, "I will never do ???? (cross country skiing for example) again!" Regardless of how harmless you might think those words are, they are a vow plain and simple. And we need to be very careful what we commit to...or who.

Jonah made a vow to the Lord then changed his mind. He decided he didn't like the assignment. After a stint in the belly of a whale for three days Jonah realized that God holds us accountable for the words we utter and the vows we commit ourselves to. But God is not the only one. Lucifer likewise holds us accountable for the vows and promises we make. Vows are verbal contracts that hold us captive to whatever was spoken. They are supernatural or spiritual power that commits us to a line of action that must be fulfilled, one way or another.

Words are power and we must use them wisely. It is perhaps one of the most difficult tasks we must master and many fail to realize its importance.

Curses are also spoken, again using the power of words. They are not only used against us by others; we curse ourselves with unwise words all the time. In days gone by (think generational, families, or war however long ago) people were more selective. Their words were used as specific weapons against enemies. These weapons were known as curses. Witch doctors, witches and priests still use curses as weapons against enemies or clients' enemies. The movie Braveheart comes to mind.

With each vow, curse, promise and dedication there is a spirit tie created. Words are power in the spiritual realm because they are spiritual in nature. We were created by the spoken word. Worlds, star systems and universes were created and are being created by the spoken word. The spoken word stops the sun for a day. The spoken word causes miracles to happen all around us. The spoken word has called out the salvation of mankind; it has called the downfall of man. The spoken word is power and supernatural realm currency.

Words are the easiest way to create spirit ties and have been used for millennia to bond children and relatives to the paths taken by their ancestors. They have bonded future generations to past words and hidden agendas. And all of this is done in the name of a god that was not the Lord Almighty, Yahweh. It was done using His name blasphemously.

Ancient curses have caused infertility, female and male anatomical problems, marital problems, early deaths, childhood maladies...all from words spoken against their perceived enemy to do harm to the family line.

Dedications to gods and priests have condemned family lines to years of misery.

Breaking off generational curses, vows, promises, dedications, etc. is equally as important as breaking off generational spirit ties. It allows us to step out from under the curse and into our inheritance, our Kingdom promises.

Exodus 20:5 tells us that the iniquity of the fathers shall be visited to the fourth generation.

How much more this applies when it is spiritual ties from curses, vows and dedications spoken by or to our ancestors. Essentially, by breaking these things off our lives, we are causing the words to fall to the ground void, removing it from the realm of active assignments.

How do these things affect our lives? My family line, called to be prophets before the Lord, was actually dedicated to Babylonian priests and Druid priests. By the time I was seven years of age, I was having visions of Babylonian rites, not realizing exactly what they were until years later. But by the time I was seven, I had my siblings and neighborhood friends walk in a *secret* procession around our house, holding aloft burning bulrushes while chanting some ancient ditty or dedication. My life was filled with similar oddities that escaped understanding until years of research later exposed the truth. I'm sure you are thinking that you have never done anything remotely so bizarre. I use my own life to make a point. There are many ungodly beliefs in every family line and religious circles that have come out of ancient rites.

Further examples of curses are barrenness, often coming from words spoken. You will find it tends to follow family lines and can be remedied by breaking the curses. How many people do you know are afraid of the water with no explanation? Chances are they are associated with an old favorite pastime of dunking "suspected" witches into the river while tied to a chair. If they survived they were innocent!

These ancient vows, promises, curses and dedications have an effect on our lives today.

Look into your generational bloodlines as best you can. Do a little Google research and see what you find. There are revealing cultural religious paradigms in the annals of history. Be creative and thorough. If there was any possibility that your ancestors may have been a part of Druid, Celtic, Samurai, Ju Ju, Buddhist, Shaman, etc. religious rites, envision what vows, curses, dedications and promises might have been made during that time. Most of these things were so integrated into the lives of the people that there was no separation; treat them as such. Our ancestors…all of them…were superstitious people who were compelled through fear to do whatever was necessary to live as peacefully as possible.

This includes selling or giving their children to prostitute temples to satisfy the gods. This includes selling or giving their children to be eunuchs to the temples or castle. This includes selling or giving their children to the priests to become proselytes or followers. This includes ancient rites performed to enter into adulthood. This includes total lifestyles that were not based on true dedication to God but fearful dedications to whatever regional gods ruled at the time.

It all involves some form of sell-out to demonic, satanic forces that needs to be broken in our lives for us to be free to worship and follow God whole-heartedly.

Father God, I repent, renounce and fall out agreement with every spirit tie created with my ancestors and that have come through the family blood line. Father, I break the power of every word spoken over my family line, every curse, vow, promise and dedication. I call them now to be null and void in my life. I command them to fall to the ground impotent, in Jesus' name. Father God, I dedicate my life anew to You. I declare now before heaven and earth that I am fully a child of God, the Creator of the universe, the only King of Kings, the Lord God Almighty. I declare now before heaven and earth that I am not affiliated in any way with the enemy of my soul, the enemy of the Lord, Lucifer and his minions. I declare that I now break every spirit tie created with or onto my ancestors. I break their power and cancel their assignment in my life and the lives of my children — the buck stops here. And every spirit of fear, stress, anxiety, intimidation, religious, cult, control and manipulation, your power is broken and your assignment is cancelled in my life and the lives of my children. In the name of Jesus, I command you to go to the pit now, where you belong.

PLEASE NOTE: The reason you can break these vows, promises, dedications and curses off your children is because these are specially put on the children by parents or others. The same rule applies: if they can be put on the children, they can then be removed from the children.

Nowhere else does this rule apply.

Chapter 7:
Familial and Familiar "Soul Ties"

These two types of spirit ties are linked together because one occasionally passes into another.

Familial spirit ties are the ties that seem to naturally occur between family members. It is the bond between parent, child and siblings. It will also widen to the extended family…relatives…grandparents, cousins, aunts and uncles.

There is a level of heart bond that is good, it is supposed to occur, but we are talking about the abnormal bonds that can occur between family members. These abnormal bonds would be things like trying to mold the child into Dad's idea of what would bring a good income, or perhaps his unrealized dream for himself. Maybe Mom feels she gave up her dreams to raise a family and wants her daughter to have a flashy career, or even Gramma sees great potential for her grandchild to be a superstar. It can also go the other way. Instead of pressure to perform, it may be an abusive situation that holds the child back.

A real life example can also be when children rule the house through parental inversion. The child becomes the parent and the parent the child. I have seen this with a friend of mine who became ill while in Kenya. Her daughter became the parent and looked after her mother simply because there was no one else available so far from home. But it carried on long after they returned to Canada and until the mother died.

Still another example, a parent who tries to make their daughter into the boy they wanted, or of course, a son into the daughter. Some parents will try to make their children into images of themselves instead of letting the child have free expression of their own God given nature. This borders on emotional, spiritual and physical abuse on many levels.

An abnormal amount of love is another clue to a familial spirit tie. An overly doting father or mother or child is a tell-tale sign. I knew of a boy who slept on the floor beside his mother's bed because she suffered from fibromyalgia. He slept there for years because he couldn't bear to be separated. He had such an abnormal doting attachment to his mother that could not be broken.

But it is not always about abnormal love. There is also abnormal anger and hate. I am not certain how it happens, but there are times when parents hate their children. I suppose it could be transferred from a bad marital relationship...or no relationship.

Sometimes children have an abnormal hatred towards their parents, aunts, uncles or grandparents. And certainly there are times when siblings have an abnormal hatred of their brothers or sisters.

Even if it is only for a short time, these emotions will trigger spirit ties between people.

Most of us have been the victims of some form of parental abuse simply because our parents did not know better, just as their parents did not know better....they did what they thought was right. Commonly people will say they had no idea their behavior/attitude would have an influence or consequence. Let's replace those examples with out Heavenly Father's example.

We parent in the way we know, the way we were parented. But they have come out of wounded environments just as we did. Let's walk in repentance and forgiveness.

Familial spirit ties can become so strong that when one of the people dies, for example a parent or child, the remaining person will see them appear after death. These are familiar spirits. Luke 16:19-31 tells us undoubtedly that the dead cannot come back unless under special dispensation from the Lord such as when Moses and Elijah appeared to Jesus on the mount of transfiguration.

A very good example of how this happens is the story of Saul and the witch of Endor in 1 Samuel 28. Saul went to seek council from her, wanting to call back the spirit of Samuel. But, of course, the witch of Endor could not do that, so instead she called up a familiar spirit that resembled Samuel.

When we have a spirit tie with family members and they die, then we are open to having a familial spirit come that resembles them. We open ourselves up to the spirit world which is very dangerous.

Spirit ties will open us up to all sorts of things that are unacceptable and unwanted. And too often we confuse the spiritual emotions these spirit ties cause to be conjured up in us, with our own normal emotions. But these spirit ties allow spirits to travel from one person to another and often the emotions and feelings of one person will travel to another. Ever wonder why you are suddenly depressed or angry? Consider those around you who might be angry or depressed. Is it possible there is a unhealthy spirit tie between you?

Father God, I repent, renounce and fall out of agreement with the spirit ties I have allowed to be created with(name names) or that I have created with (name names). Father God, I repent, renounce and fall out of agreement with every spirit I have allowed to come through those spirit ties. Father God, I repent of every abnormal emotion of love, anger, hatred, rejection, etc. that I have felt towards another, and I repent of every abnormal feeling I have allowed to be attached to my life from another. Father God, I break the power and cancel the assignment of every spirit tie I have made with (name names) and every spirit tie I have allowed to be made with me from (name names). Father God, every spirit of fear, stress, anxiety, rejection, abnormal love, abnormal doting, anger, hatred (be creative here and express everything that you feel might be invasive)—I break their power and cancel their assignment in my life, and I command you now, in the name of Jesus, to go to the pit where you belong. Holy Spirit, I ask that you rise up and heal my heart from all the wounds and hurt that has taken hold of me. Holy Spirit, pour the balm of Gilead into my spirit and heal me; pour the balm of Gilead into my soul and heal me; pour the balm of Gilead into my body and heal me. Father, You have never rejected me. You have never loved me with abnormal love and demands. You have never hated me. You have never thrown me away. Heal my heart and give to me a revelation of Your love and life. In Jesus' most precious and holy name, amen.

Chapter 8:
Animal "Soul Ties"

This is one spirit tie I understand painfully well. Because of my isolation from family and friends, I formed attachments to my animals to feel less alone. They became my family and friends. Through these spirit ties I could always know immediately what their needs were, what their behavior meant. I could read every nuance because I could hear every thought. People think animals are mindless, that they operate on instinct alone, but each one has their own personality and special way. After all, God created each of them as well. Unfortunately, my animals and I shared some personality.

It is assumed that a horse or a dog, because of higher intelligence, is more likely to create a spirit tie than a cat, lizard, fish, etc., but the spirit tie is created because of two emotions. On the part of the human, it is created by love or control, and from the pet's perspective, it is created by dependence. When we are the sole source of their food, comfort, and care, an animal will create one or more spirit ties with their keeper.

When an animal becomes the main source of our comfort, humans will trigger spirit ties with their pets.

Both are equally dangerous, equally sinful, always playing with fire.

My poor little poodle developed the very illnesses my mother had and eventually was put on the same medications as my mother. And all that took place in less than one month. From a healthy miniature poodle, he developed thyroid problems and eventually Cushing's disease in less than thirty days because he met my mother and became completely bonded to her. They were inseparable since they day they met. I still remember the day. I came home from work and found my poodle upstairs, sitting on the love seat on his bum, legs spread out leaning his back against the arm, chowing down on a plate of real cream puffs, my mother sitting in exactly the same position on the other end. They began to look alike. They were completely dedicated to each other in every way.

My poodle eventually died of Cushing's disease, a disease caused by the spirit of fear, a mere eight years later, five to six years earlier than he should have died, and not long after she died.

That is what a spirit tie can do to our pets. That is why they can become so in tune with their owner, and so control a household. Spiritual connections.

We have experienced easier success with animal ministry than human ministry that is, delivering animals from the spirits that plague them. This is because there is no hidden agenda or hidden sins in an animal. They, like the whole earth, groan for the revealing of the sons of God so that they can be delivered and free. There is instant change in their lives, their health, and their behavior. But it took me several years to learn that they can be delivered just like us.

I am going to insert a little diversion in the area of animals here that may surprise you. I am talking about yoga and martial arts. Many of these practices from the eastern cultures take on animal forms in the practice of their spiritual exercise. I call it spiritual exercise because there is always a religious connotation associated with these practices. Assuming the animal position in both disciplines is a matter of claiming the strength and peace of the animal, bringing that energy or spirit into the practitioner's life. The instructor may, or may not teach you this.

In essence, this is simply the practice of connecting to a spirit that is representing an animal, then opening the door to create a spirit tie with that spiritual "animal". Voila, you have a spirit tie with a demonic dog, cat, lion...whatever. Nonetheless, a demonic spirit.

The same principle applies to spirit guides, tree worship, or animal worship (cows, rats, frogs, whatever), vegetable or natural creature. It is creating a spirit tie with the spirit that is either hiding in that creature or has taken the form of said creature. We open ourselves to invite that spirit into our lives.

Spirits are bodiless fallen angels and are no longer in the kingdom of God, but are found in the kingdom of Satan. It is not a difficult thing to be freed from these misconceptions. It does require a decision to turn from sin, break the spirit tie and a cast out the spirit. Once again, satan has lied, manipulated, and coerced throughout millennia to blind us to his tactics. The gig is up. God is revealing much deception. Exposing the enemy and seeing the truth are a major part of the battle. All that's left is to just say "NO".

In the case of breaking the spirit tie off pets and animals, you must remember, as with children and people, to break the spirit tie off both ends. We do this so that the tide of spirits does not tsunami back onto the other person or animal. It's like an umbilical cord. After it is cut from the mother, it will fall from the baby because there is no longer a need to be connected, in this case a need to be connected by these spirit beings.

Father God, I repent, renounce and fall out of agreement with every spirit tie with (name names) I have created or have allowed to be created with me. Father God, I repent, renounce and fall out of agreement with every spirit tie I have created with a yogic (Hindu god) or martial art animal form and the spirit involved with that animal form. Father God, forgive me for not knowing what I was doing. In the name of Jesus, I break the power and cancel the assignment of every spirit tie; I break them on both ends and I break the power and cancel the assignment of every spirit that came through these spirit ties. And in the name of Jesus, I cast them into the pit where they belong. Holy Spirit, I ask You to rise up and fill every cell that was inhabited by these spirits. I ask for peace in this matter. I ask for comfort in this matter. Father God, forgive me my indiscretion and sin and heal my heart, in the name of Jesus.

Chapter 9:
Idol "Soul Ties"

This is not only a generational problem; it is a growing current problem. We might laugh at the concept of our children having idols, but it is a real concern and danger in some cases. Some children experience personality and habit changes due to their idol worship. I know of one woman who went so far as to change her name legally to the name of her idol.

Idols come in many different forms. They can be cartoon or puppet characters, invisible friends, fantasy characters, teachers, peers in school, church or any social outlet, or heroes...television, music, sport, book or movie heroes.

It seems to be human nature to need someone to emulate. Of course, in theory, this should be Jesus, but that is rarely the case. Even among Christians, the more common response is to emulate other Christians. People they think appear holy or have a special talent or even look that is desirable.

We were never meant to emulate any man, woman, child, fantasy character or animal. We were meant to be our own individual person and become more God-like in our attitudes and habits, to love ourselves as we have been created. Sometimes it takes courage to be individual in this world of conformity.

Idols come in all forms for all different reasons. But in every case they create a barrier between the person and God. Without fail, anything that comes before God will interfere with a person's walk and faith.

They can range from a cartoon character to a rock star. They can be a church leader. They can be a teacher, even a school-yard bully. They can be anyone or anything that illicit undue adulation, increasing to an unreasonable level over time.

It may start out with posters, pictures, T-shirts or lunch boxes but can end up with personality changes, mood swings and a sense of loss of reality. Or in some cases, the "idol" may be an integral part of your daily life.

In ancient times, idols were stone, bone, metal or wooden carvings that represented gods, demons, angels and kings or emperors. People emulated their supposed traits with wild, abandoned sexual practices, drunken orgies, cuttings, piercings and tattooing. These practices eventually led the worshipper into murdering their own offspring as offerings and platitudes to a demanding deity.

In every culture on earth, these cults demanded animal and human sacrifice to their god or deity especially in desperate times needing change. Sacrifice of something or someone was always a way to placate an angry deity and perhaps win their favor.

In contrast, the God of the Christian faith is the only God that gave the life of His own Son as sacrifice for the sins of man. No other god in any culture ever sacrificed their own life or the life of their only begotten Son to pay for the sins of the worshippers.

The large, bulky idols gave way to smaller carvings or talismans who were worshipped with no less piety and devotion. Small stone carvings, stone circles, trees, etc. became the symbols of worship during the time of the Celts and Druids. The Japanese wore magic mirrors around their necks that held the hidden image of their god. Most African, Native American cultures wore a talisman sack around their neck. Oriental cultures wore talismans carved of jade around their necks or wrists. All demanded some form of sacrifice from the worshipper.

In more severe religions, the dedications, however, were more horrific. Not only were children dedicated to their gods, but entire generational lines were dedicated to the worship of their gods as in the case of British Druids and European Celts.

It was revealed to me in vision that my own generational line had been dedicated to Druids, complete with the Old Way teachings that went clear back to the Middle East and Mlk (Moloch) teachings.

Idol worship has deep generational spirit ties that span dedications, vows and promises made by our ancestors. These promises, dedications and vows are surprisingly binding and provide legal ground for demonic possession. These generational lines need to be broken.

It is common place these days for men and women to envision their current idols while having sex with their spouses. It may seem like a small thing, but this is the same as adultery according to the Bible.

We have come to accept things that are totally unacceptable because "everybody's doing it", and the apparent lack of retribution. Things that are common become acceptable. We lose our children to the people they idolize because they no longer respect their parents. We have lost our children to outside sources, being influenced by people who have extremely questionable habits. Rock stars and movie stars epitomize drugs, illicit affairs, provocative dress code, and abuse...they are raising our children. They are usually people we would not want our children to be like; however, we do not stop their growing infatuation. Indeed, many of us share the same infatuations with our kids. Standards, God's plum line have been trampled underfoot.

Each infatuation creates a spirit tie. It is very simple. The intense emotion or repetitive observance triggers the spirit within to create a spirit tie with the object of our affection. That spirit tie, say with a rock star, allows the spirits of that rock star to enter the child, teen or adult and the spirits of the person enter the rock star. It is a major freeway between the observer and idol. It causes the observer to get tattoos or piercings to be just like their hero. They might begin to dress the same or in similar fashion. They distance themselves from their family the more they are drawn into their idol. Prevalent examples are gothic and punk styles.

This is what fuels cults and religious groups. The devotee will sacrifice everything to become like their idol. Whether this is done through coercion or willingness does not matter, the outcome is the same. Spirit ties need to be broken to break the connection, to cut the control. Without the spirit ties broken, the initiate will always be connected to the leader in question, and unable to see the irrational hold or influence.

This same principle applies in any situation of total unquestioning submission; rock stars, movie stars, peers, persons in authority, etc. The spirit tie that connects the two together must be eliminated. Then, of course, every spirit that has come through the tie must be sent to the pit.

If you are wondering why we send spirits to the pit it is because they are bound in the pit for one thousand years. But nowhere in the Bible does it say that God or the angels will put the spirits into the pit. It does say that we are to be delivered. I was chastised three years ago because I was not sending the spirits to the pit after being told to do so. It took two years for me to remember. Now I send every spirit to the pit. We are to clean the earth of their influence and their presence in obedience, just like the angels themselves threw the rebels out of heaven. The sin in the camp needs to be obliterated. Now they will be trapped and bound in the pit for one thousand years according to scripture.

Again, the same applies to spirit guides. The spirit ties must be broken for the initiate to be free of that religion and spirit guide.

Father God, I repent, renounce and fall out of agreement with every spirit tie I have created or allowed to be created with an idol: a being or object that I have placed before You in my life. Father, I repent for everything I have allowed to get in the way of my relationship with You. I fall out of agreement with everything I have allowed to sit upon the throne of my heart in Your place. Lord, I take them off the throne and place You on the throne of my heart, Your rightful place. Lord I bow my knee to You and claim that You are Lord of my life. I declare before heaven and earth that there is no one else that is king of my life. Only You the Lord God, Almighty, Yahweh is His name. I declare now, before heaven and earth that the Lord my God, the Lord is One. I break off every spirit tie created with (name names). I break their power and cancel their assignment in my life. And every spirit that came through these soul ties, your power is broken and your assignment is cancelled in my life and in the name of Jesus, I command you to go to the pit where you will be held for one thousand years. Holy Spirit, I ask You to rise up within me and heal every wound and connection point of the spirit ties so that there is nothing left. Heal my heart, Lord, heal my heart. In Jesus' most holy and precious name I ask to be freed of these idols so that I can worship and praise the Lord God Almighty in purity and wholeness. Lord, release and set me free in You to be free to be with You. Lord, heal me and release me in Jesus' name, amen.

Chapter 10:
Spirit "Soul Ties"

Essentially all spirit ties are made by spirits on the unction of either a person experiencing strong emotion (fear, guilt, anger etc.), or one spirit (in a person) with a spirit in the other person. Spirits do not perform the act of creating a tie simply because they know the mechanics of this method of bondage but do so because the person they inhabit provides an open door.

Every person is born with spirits already at work in them because they are generationally inherited. Other spirits are picked up through the parents familiarly and through the consent of their own actions.

People are natural beings with spiritual authority in Christ through the power of their voice but they do not have the ability to manipulate the spiritual kingdom to serve their own agendas. Spirits, however, can manipulate the spiritual laws, working within them, to serve their own agendas because they understand those spiritual laws.

With this in mind, the most devastating of all spirit ties occur when the person is attached directly to a spirit/fallen angel/demon. Regardless of what name you use, the entity is the same, as are the evil intentions towards you.

People in every culture throughout history have ceremonially and willingly attached themselves to spirits one way or another. There are ceremonies of dedication that involve drugs, cutting, piercings, hanging (suspended by hooks) and tattoos. People work themselves into trances using mantras, music, dances, hypnosis, drugs, chanting, starvation, etc. They do all this for the dubious glory of binding themselves with an evil entity who will control their every thought, action and movement from the moment of connection.

There is an excellent example in 1Kings 18 where Elijah is competing with the priests of Baal to see whose God is greater. Elijah relaxes at his altar while the priests of Baal work themselves into a frenzy; chanting, dancing and cutting themselves to no avail. They attached themselves to spirits represented by a stone statue called Baal. Baal had no power because he was simply a statue. The spirits had power in the spiritual world but they could not cause fire to come down and lap up the offering of wood in the natural world. It was not that they were prevented by Yahweh to set fire to the wood, but they were simply not capable of such a feat.

We give these spirits too much credit in relationship. They have only the authority we relinquish to them, no more.

Their power lay in their ability to cause the priests to mutilate themselves and others in the name of their god. Their power lay in their ability to get Jezebel to kill all the followers and prophets of Yahweh. Their power lay in their ability to control the one they were attached to, who gave them permission for control. And their power lay in the fear that came upon the people as they watched all of these things.

Yahweh's power lays in the fact that He not only created everything and everyone, but that He controls everything in the natural and spiritual universe. His power lays in the fact that He is God. His power lays in the fact that He created the control of everything that is His alone.

If you attach yourself to a statue, picture, carving, caricature, relief or fact simile of anything or anyone, you are attaching your affections to that spirit. A spirit tie is created allowing a wide open door for any spirit to enter into you.

If you have a spirit tie with a person and that person dies, you now have inherited a spirit tie with the spirit that was in that person, which again is another open door for any spirit to enter into you. The same concept holds true with a pet or idol. If the pet or idol (hero) dies, it is another open door for the spirit that possessed that pet or idol (hero). If there is a connection with an idol, as in a representation of a god, then there is a direct connection with the spirit that statue represents. The same law applies to Ouija boards, tarot cards, bones, etc.

The mechanics are simple. If you have a spirit tie with a person, pet or idol (hero) that is alive, you are limited to receive only the spirits that person, pet or idol have. However, when they die and that spirit tie is attached to a spirit alone, then you are open to receive any spirit they give permission to enter the spirit tie. And they give permission to every spirit because they can.

Tattoos and piercings are decorative in today's society, but their roots are far from attractive.

Let's use the example I saw on TV of a man devastated by his wife's death. He wanted her image tattooed onto his chest over his heart. Now, if you get a tattoo to represent a person who has died, you are marking your body with a representation of a spirit tie which allows any spirit to enter. Adding to the depth of this poor man's spiritual bondage he wanted her ashes mixed into the ink used to pierce his skin. He now has every spiritual connection she lived with willingly inserted into his own flesh. This opened him up to a multitude of spirit ties, more than he originally had with her. He had no idea there was more at play than love and respect for his wife that caused him to think this was a good way to honor her.

Piercing, scarring, burning and cutting accomplish the same thing. Exodus 21:2-6 explains that piercing your ear with an awl is the sign of your commitment to life-long slavery. But even worse, it is the sign that displays you have been set free from servant status and now choose instead to remain as slave. It is an unchangeable sign. The mark remains after death.

We take these things so casually because they have become part of our culture. But perhaps we should look at the origins of these practices before we condone them for ourselves or our children. The origins of all these practices have a spiritual impact on our lives.

Makeup, for example, was begun so that when people looked into a mirror they saw themselves through the image of Isis, their goddess, proving that they were one with their goddess.

We need to be more careful what we open ourselves up to, and because it is culturally accepted does not negate the spiritual impact that may occur. This is especially true in the present day because the origins are long forgotten.

Burning began by branding a person or animal as property or as an outcast or criminal. I could be wrong, but it seems to me that one of the first places one could get a tattoo in the western world was in prison. Piercing began as a sign of declared slavery. Scarring began as spiritual decoration to invite magick into one's life. Tattoos began the same way as scarring, as magical talismans to protect the wearer against harm and disease or pain.

The oldest tattooed person is carbon dated to be five thousand years old and was discovered on a mountain between Austria and Italy. His skin bears fifty-seven tattoos including a cross behind his left knee. The position of the tattoos suggests that they were applied for medical reasons to combat something, maybe arthritis.

In 1948, a group of kurgans were excavated in the Altai mountain range of south-western Siberia. The mummies found in the tombs had tattoos of animals and griffins (body of a lion with wings and head of an eagle) that held magical significance for the culture.

In Egypt, women priestesses of Hathor bore geometric tattoos. In Japan, clay figurines served as stand-ins for living individuals who symbolically accompanied the dead on their journey into the unknown. These figurines were covered with tattoo marks that had religious and magical power. Tattoos have been found in China, India, Polynesia, Hawaii, Indonesia, New Zealand, Thailand, Africa, ancient Greece and Rome, among the Celts, in Central and South America, North America, the Vikings, Middle East, England and France. They were used for religious, magical and decorative purposes, but their beginning intent was always to evoke magick into a person's life.

The life of the flesh is in the blood (Leviticus 17:11). Because of this, the blood is highly valued in the occult as the power source of life. By releasing or *letting* the blood, the supernatural power is unleashed. Cutting the flesh and blood letting are rituals that have been performed throughout history to unleash demonic and supernatural power. The kids who do this say they are hurting themselves so they do not have to hurt someone else!!

Mark 5 tells us the story of the man of Gadarenes who was possessed by an unclean spirit. He could be bound by no man and he hid in the tombs crying and *cutting himself.* Cutting of oneself is the result of a spirit tie with, and possession by, an unclean spirit. In this case, a complete legion of them, which is numbered between 4,500 and 6,000 spirits.

The spirit tie must all be broken and the spirit cast out for the person to find peace. Jesus cast out the spirits of Legion from the man, spirits that came in through spirit ties with some source. I must wonder, as the story goes on, if the spirit ties were not with the pigs. Because, from personal experience,

I know the spirits flow from the person who has just cut the tie to the thing or person at the other end of the spirit tie. And considering pigs were unclean animals to the Hebrews, and he had unclean spirits, it is quite possible that there were religious or financial ties with the pigs we might not understand.

It is quite possible that the man from Gadarenes was a powerful business man, trading in pigs before insanity reigned in him. Could it be why the townspeople had either fear or respect for him and tried to contain him rather than killing him for his crimes against them?

Stretching a part of the body containing cartilage has existed for thousands of years. Stretched earlobes began in China, while stretched lip piercings began in Africa and South America. Others today include tongue stretching, lip plates, and septum stretching. Today all these forms are called body mutilation or body sculpting. It is a growing phenomenon around the world. These stretching or body mutilations are the same as cutting; they are mutilating the body for decoration or dedication.

All of it says that we are not pleased with the appearance God created, in His likeness. Like Lucifer, we have to make God's creation better. In ancient times, this was done to identify oneself with one's god or spirit guide.

But there are more ways these spirit ties are released into action. Old cultures such as the Native American culture often talk about the young feeling the pull of the unseen elders. The same is true in every original culture worldwide, such as the

Maoris, Aborigines, etc. These cultures invoke spiritual associations to enact the spirit tie with their younger generation. This is done in special ceremonies that have been performed for millennia. These spirit ties have to be broken for the children to be free from the hold of the elders.

There is a religious organization that baptizes their converts as they examine family lines and genealogies. This act of baptizing, since it is not of God or God-ordained, is a satanic act, yet another perversion. How do I know this? Nowhere in the Bible is there a mandate for baptism of the deceased family lines or persons who are not aware they are taking part in the ritual.

There are spirit ties created between satanic cults, covens, etc. with the people living in the vicinity. This is used to create a hedge of protection for the cult member. It is used as a means to control the situations of the neighbors around the area. These are real things that need to be considered. Christians should not be naïve or ignorant of the things of the spiritual world that lies around them. It makes them as sheep in a wolf's den and we are told to be wise as serpents.

Christians need to become aware of the spiritual world and how it works. How can you fight the war if you do not know your enemy's location and tactics? Jesus has given us the authority and the tools, but if we do not pick them up and know how to use them, we lose the advantage.

Father God, I repent, renounce and fall out of agreement with every spirit I have created a spirit tie with or allowed them to create a spirit tie with me. Lord God, make known to me specifically those things that need to be broken, or if I need to break them individually. Lord, I want to be free of every spirit tie that has me bogged down. Father, I cry out to be free! Help me be free. Show me that which has me bound and free me from its control. I stand before heaven and earth as a child of the Most High God, the Father Almighty who created heaven and earth. I declare I am no longer connected with the spiritual realm of fallen angels and false gods. Father God, I want to be free from all ties and bonds that have been created outside of You. In the name of Jesus, I break the power of every spirit tie and cancel its assignment in my life. Every spirit of control, manipulation, fear, stress and anxiety, oppression and depression, and every spirit of (be creative and name names here), I break its power and cancel its assignment in my life. Father God, I declare that I am free in the name of Jesus. I command every spirit named and unnamed, works with, associated with and affiliated with to go to the pit, in the name of Jesus, and get out of my life. Holy Spirit, I ask that you rise up and heal every wound, every connection, and every point of contact. Heal me in every cell. In the name of Jesus, I speak healing and health to my body, soul and spirit. Holy Spirit, I ask that You clean off every mark from my spirit so that I am no longer a target for these spirit ties. Wash my spirit clean, in the name of Jesus. I apply the blood of Jesus to every cell, tissue and part of my body and I command that my body work the way it was designed to work, in the name of Jesus. Again, I ask You to reveal to me every tie that needs to be broken individually. Reveal everything that is hidden from me so that I can be free. Free my spirit to serve You, Lord, for I have no other master than You. I declare before heaven and earth that there is only one God and His name is Yahweh, Yeshua and Holy Spirit and He is my God. I serve no other gods and I break their power and tie with me, in the name of Jesus. I declare I am free in Jesus' name, amen.

Chapter 11:
Telltale Signs of "Soul Ties"

Two decades ago I decided to sell colored garbage bags. We used, as our logo, a caricature of me as *a bag lady*, which was the name of our company, complete with shopping cart. But things suddenly turned sour for me. Everything I put my hand to failed. That caricature hung in my bathroom for fifteen years because I liked it, until the Lord finally had me throw it out and break off the spirit ties with the picture and what it represented. Once that was done, I then cast out the spirits of poverty and failure. Since that time, things have turned around for me financially as well as spiritually.

These spirit ties can happen innocently enough, but that does not impede the intended purpose for them. The spiritual effect and impact on our lives have been assigned and will continue until we step up to expose and remove our enemy's plan. We must be sensitive to the Holy Spirit to root out the things in our lives that are holding us back from the blessings of the Lord. The Lord has given each one of us an inheritance that has carried through our generations…but wasn't picked up by our ancestors. That does not mean the inheritance has disappeared; it is just waiting for someone to pick it up. But if we are not walking in our inheritance, then something in our lives is standing in the way. We need to be sensitive to the Holy Spirit to find out just what that might be. You will find that the very things you have been plagued with are carefully selected to keep you from your intended inheritance.

Spirit ties can happen for many reasons. To further illustrate the many ways they might be created, I will try to show some examples of seemingly innocent approaches I have encountered.

Often, as we travel, we purchase local carvings, masks, dolls or wall hangings. Although, most times, they are simply decoration, often they have been prayed over and dedicated to the gods they were created to represent. In fact, some even go so far as to put curses on the very items they sell to make a living. It is a familiar belief that if you do not agree with my beliefs, then you are a danger to me.

For an unwary traveler, that little souvenir is enough to create a spirit tie with the spirit world, opening their life and their home up to any number of spiritual attacks. You may think this is overkill, but I have personally heard too many stories of people's behavior changing, or their circumstances unexplainably altered after an artifact is purchased or received as a gift. After much prayer, the Lord revealed the source of the problem which in one case was simply a bowl from a native South American culture.

The spirit world uses our lack of knowledge as an effective weapon against us. We need to clean our homes and the things in it, either through prayer or perhaps getting rid of the object in question as well. There is a reason the Bible tells us not to make images resembling an animal or any part of creation for decoration in our homes. It was said to be a safety net for unwary sheep who haven't thought about the spiritual consequences.

ক৵৵৶

I had an anger problem for over fifty years. In the last twelve years I have delivered spirits of anger and rage countless times, but my blood pressure was still out of control and the anger always just lurking. My doctors were so concerned that they wanted to hospitalize me to get my pressure under control. But then the Lord revealed to me that the reason the anger and rage remained within me was because I had not gotten to the root of the problem.

The root was revealed in vision. Apparently, one of my ancestors sacrificed her four-year-old daughter on an altar in a Slovenian cave. As you might guess, neither the mother nor the daughter was pleased and thus a dual-root for the rage and anger developed. The spirit ties were no longer attached to the ancestors, of course, but they were attached to the spirits represented by the ancestors.

Before the root could be broken, I actually had to stand in the place of both mother and child. As the child, I had to forgive the mother for sacrificing me. And as the mother, I had to forgive myself for sacrificing my daughter for spiritual power. The very moment I repented and forgave, the spirit of anger was broken and it left. The root was broken and forgiveness was given. I prayed for the spirit ties to be broken and every spirit of fear, stress, anxiety, anger and rage to be broken and their assignment cancelled in my life. My blood pressure returned to below normal and I have not suffered from that long-term anger and rage for over a year now.

The Bible tells us that the sins of the father will carry through until the fourth generation. This does not mean the sins of the mother do not carry forward. And it does mean that the sin carries forward as part of our DNA unless there is repentance. It will stand in the way of us picking up our inheritance. Ask the Lord to restore your DNA structure to reflect His design, His genetics for you.

ᴖᴄ

When a person goes to a horror movie, it is a ready vehicle for spirit ties to be connected. When there is a sudden surge of fright or anxiety, it is an open door for a spirit tie to be formed between the viewer and the spirit portrayed by the movie. The emotion hits suddenly which causes a trauma to the innocence of our soul. That trauma opens up a doorway for a spirit of fear to enter. That spirit of fear creates a spirit tie with the spirit behind the image or sound on the screen. That spirit tie allows that image to be replayed over and over again in our dreams, causing sleepless nights and nightmares. It many cases, the spirit of fear will haunt us at every opportunity.

The trauma has to be closed, the spirit of fear has to be broken and it's assignment cancelled, the spirit tie has to be broken and the spirit of nightmares and fear have to broken and cancelled in our lives. Everything has to be thrown into the pit in the name of Jesus. Ask the Holy Spirit to bring peace to your spirit and soul and apply the blood of Jesus to the images you have seen to cleanse them from your mind. It is just that quick and easy.

୧ଡ଼ଡ଼

One day, I was taking a shower while house sitting. I was suddenly attacked with the fear that someone was standing on the other side of the shower curtain. I was so overcome with fear that I couldn't even move the curtain to check. I prayed against the fear, but still I was certain that someone was on the other side of the curtain. You could not have convinced me otherwise. However, with great struggle, I got hold of myself and opened the curtain. No one was there. It was not until sometime later that I discovered that the lady in the apartment below had an uncontrollable fear of this very same thing. I broke off the spirit tie created by her and cast out the spirits to the pit and have never been bothered since.

If you experience overwhelming emotions that you know are simply not yours, they may be transferring to you through a spirit tie with someone who has those feelings.

୧ଡ଼ଡ଼

My mother read so many true crime books that she created a spirit tie with the spirit of fear. She would wake up in the middle of the night hearing people walking down the hallway. She began to smell atrocities in her bedroom that drove her to great agitation. She could no longer stay home alone. She had a particular passion for one true crime writer and created a spirit tie with her.

To be free, she only had to break off the trauma of the words from her soul, break off the power and cancel the assignment in her life. She only had to break off the power of the spirit tie in her, breaking the power and cancelling the assignment of the legion of fear, stress and anxiety in her life. She only had to ask the Holy Spirit to give her peace. But instead, she died of fear and stress related disease just a few years before I began to discover the simple remedy to be free of these plagues of terror.

ை

Many people with chronic or acute illnesses become so dependant on their doctors they will develop spirit ties making them feel safer. The relationship becomes almost intimate in familiarity. Although this may seem like an extension of trust, in reality it is taking God out of the equation and opening the door for all the issues from the doctor and his family tree. We must exercise caution in this area. The same things can happen with nurses or other care givers we become dependent on if even for a short time.

ை

In the case of assault, the mechanics are again simple. A person trapped by the fear of being hurt again, of constantly expecting an attack, cannot be free unless they break the spirit tie created at the moment of the assault.

When a person is assaulted, at the very moment the pain is felt, at the very moment of the trauma of the pain, a spirit tie is created with the person who causes the pain. A clearer picture is that at the moment of impact of a fist, the victim will create a spirit tie with the fist that has caused the pain of the blow. At the moment the pain is felt, the door of trauma is opened and a spirit of fear and pain enter. A spirit tie is created with the attacker and this creates a continual flinch or fear of being struck in the same spot. It happens within a millisecond but can last a lifetime.

In the case of a rape, there is a slight difference. The attack usually lasts much longer and is so intense that there is not one spirit tie, but several. The same situation applies with a prolonged beating when someone is beaten severely.

At the moment of the trauma, and every new trauma inflicted, a spirit tie with the rapist is created. It is very difficult, and in some cases nearly impossible, for a rape victim to overcome their rape. The fear, uncleanness, anger...they all remain. There is not one tie to deal with, but several, and the spirits that entered through each tie. When these ties are broken and the spirits' power broken and their assignment cancelled in the life of the victim, the heart can finally begin to heal. I will include a prayer at the end of this chapter for rape victims.

∽✍

There are many symptoms of spirit ties.

1.   There is a spirit tie present when one person is obsessed with another person, pet or thing. The person obsessed cannot get the other person out of their minds.

2. There is a spirit tie present when one person knows the thoughts of another.

3. There is a spirit tie present when one person knows where another person is at all times.

4. There is a spirit tie present when there is still a "ping" when you think of someone or an incident. If there is still a rise of anger or emotion, the spirit tie is still present.

5. There is a spirit tie present if one person feels they are being watched or are not alone.

6. There is a spirit tie present when there has been deliverance for a specific issue, example grief, and that issue has not been resolved.

7. There is a spirit tie present when there is overwhelming fear that cannot be overcome.

Father God, I repent, renounce and fall out of agreement with every spirit tie I created with my rapist. Father, forgive me for reaching out in a time of desperation and linking to the very person who was hurting me. Father, I break every spirit tie created, one for every moment of the attack, one for every new wave of humiliation and fear. Father God, I break every spirit tie on both sides. I break the power and cancel the assignment of every spirit that came through those ties, every spirit of rape, fear, stress, anxiety, pain, humiliation, uncleanness, control, manipulation, power, sadism, horror, powerless-ness, victim, shame (name all you feel), and in the name of Jesus I command every spirit named to be cast into the pit where you belong. Leave me now.

Father, I pray for my heart that has been shattered and damage by this betrayal. Holy Spirit, I ask that You go and retrieve the shards of my heart that have splintered and been taken by my rapists, and I ask that You return the parts of his heart that have been left in me. Father, I pray for wholeness and healing. Pour the balm of Gilead into my heart and heal it from the inside out. Pour the balm of Gilead into my heart until overflowing so the healing is complete and swift. Pour the balm of Gilead into my heart and heal it from the inside out, removing all scars and marks upon my heart. Lord, God Almighty, rise up and heal my heart and my life, my soul and my spirit. Holy Spirit I ask that You remove all the marks off my spirit, soul and body and make me a clean vessel. Remove the memory and touch of my rapist. Replace his touch with Your comfort; replace his smell with the Holy smell of Your mercy and love. I apply the blood of Jesus to the memory and ask that it be purged from my mind and my heart.

Father, clean me from head to foot, from the inside out. Make me whole and complete in You. I ask for a revelation of Your love for me, Your acceptance of me, Your longing for me. I ask for a revelation of how You feel about me and see me.

In Jesus' precious name, amen.

Chapter 12:
Legal Ground for "Soul Ties"

It is imperative to understand the function and subtle workings of demonic spirit ties in our lives, in our generations, and in our world.

Maybe you have broken off some of these spirit ties and it keeps reforming, or the problem persists, you will need to seek the Lord to reveal the legal ground. This is the incident or encounter that opened the door giving them the right to remain. They are totally legalistic in nature. Sometimes it is ancient, sometimes it is in your own lifetime, perhaps just forgotten, or maybe you consider it insignificant. It may very well be something you no longer consider important, but still the door was opened and the connection to the spirit realm established. Ask the Holy Spirit to lead you to the moment of entry so you are able to break the hold. Sometimes, unless you/Holy Spirit exposes the entry point, they will cling to the belief that they have a legal right to stay. The blood of Jesus will break the tie and even remove the infestation, but you remain vulnerable if the entry point remains open. Close doors, break traumas, and take a close look around you. It may be that you are exposed every day to the source. A work relationship, a home relationship where tension or disagreements are common may be your trigger point. You cannot always change the circumstances but you can take charge of your spiritual environment. What is bound in heaven can be bound on earth. Cancel assignments against you in Jesus name…as often as it takes.

Finding these entry points of legal ground is not always easy or straight forward. You may have to dig a little, be creative in thinking about your ancestry. Consider where your family originated. If you have no idea who your ancestors are, do a study on first and last names. Take into account the most logical origins of your name, by using the things you do know about your family.

I know very little about my family except that my father was Irish and my mother's mother was German, and her father was Scottish. Considering my last name is Jones, I know that my father's true line is from Wales. Looking into the history of Ireland, I know that the Irish stole children from Wales, Scotland, England and Spain to be their slaves. My father's family was very likely one of these children from Wales. I can then break off the spirit of poverty and servanthood by dealing with that assignment of slavery and poverty that existed in my family line. Add to this that my father was sold to a farmer at the age of nine, I know that there is an issue of slavery that runs through my father's line. I can also look at the Celtic believes of earth and element worship.

Looking back to the historical records of the dispersal of mankind, and at the family traits I share, I can trace my family line from the Hittites, through Slovenia, France, Germany, England and Ireland. I can follow the most logical religious affiliations and practices. I can make assumptions based on what feels right with my spirit. And of course, it never hurts to go overboard. If in doubt, cast it out!

One doesn't need any other ability than to be able to know when the Holy Spirit witnesses to something you read or study. It is the Holy Spirit's job to route these things out of your life. It is your job to be open to what the Holy Spirit says and follow His leading. Remember, Jesus provided the keys. We need to put it in the door and turn it.

This is a pursuit to get clean and free from the chains that Lucifer puts around us. He has been on the job for 6,000 years. It is time for him to be deposed. Jesus has paid our ransom...let's not waste one precious drop. One must be diligent and faithful to not only get rid of the spirit ties that exist but also prevent new ones from attaching. After a bit of practice, you will quickly recognize the signs. It takes less than a minute to clear things away and free yourself from any new bonds. Make it part of your daily prayer/devotions.

Legal ground is the foot hold found in the events of our ancestry, whether we like to think that or not. Everything not of God's nature that has snuck into our life must be put at the foot of the cross, under the blood of Jesus. Jesus sacrificed His life on our behalf, but we must appropriate His sacrifice and apply it to every part of our life. This includes every issue that still plagues us. Let Him live in every room of His temple...our bodies. It is after all, His body.

If we are not walking in the full nature of the Father who created us, then we have issues that need to be revealed, removed and life restored. And these issues are not always what they seem. Some may be written in our DNA which cannot be rewritten until cleansing occurs, that is by removing the spirit ties that hold them in place. It is a simple matter to remove any spirit tie discovered and restore the God ordained DNA.

Sometimes a legal tie will not be broken because we really want to keep it – it has become familiar, comfortable. A good example of this is a religious spirit. Its very nature wants control, and as it controls the host, the host gains control of those around them. People tend to want to maintain that control.

This is also often because we have been taught, and believe, that there are Godly soul ties. However, this is absolutely not the truth. There can be love without spirit ties and there is definitely Godly love. However, spirit ties are created because of a controlling emotion and this would include an obsessive, controlling love. Which of course is not love at all. Obsession never involves God. Soul ties never involve God. The Holy Spirit is the only connection we need to one another.

As I mentioned, anyone teaching Godly soul ties has no experience, understanding the true nature of spirit ties; I am sorry to say that I have been there. However, I am grateful that the Father allowed that period in my life for such a time as this. To reveal and expose the most sabotaging, insidious tactic of the enemy of our souls.

Break all spirit ties, and keep diligently on top of them until you feel free from their influence and hold. God bless you.

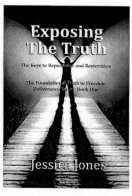

Exposing the truth compares the heart of God to the reality of present day Christianity.

Exposing The Truth examines how far we have fallen from the life and world God intended for His Bride. It documents the progress of continual falling of man after the fall of the man! Studying God's plan for His Creation, we then can see what has followed throughout the 6,000 years. The misconceptions, the lies that have shaped our lives on earth. Even as Christians we struggle to keep our relationship with God alive, and especially to move into a deeper relationship with Him. Christians struggle to keep those communication lines open, believing God must not be on the job, when in reality, the problem is our lack of understanding or knowledge of our Father, God.

This book endeavors to break out of the boxed-in mindset we have inherited...not our Godly inheritance, but our satanic inheritance. It looks into the varied world structures of our current societies, attempting to expose the truth of their origins. By Exposing the Truth in relation to our current life situation regardless of our geographical roots, it becomes evident how far off the mark of Christ Jesus we have traveled. It's time to get back on track.

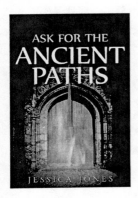

Ask for the Ancient Paths is an amazing, life-changing vision that takes you on the journey from before time through the end of this age. It shows how the jealousy of one angel forever marred the life of every angel and man alike.

This vision reveals aspects of three heavens, hell and that will forever change the way you look at the supernatural world. Follow through this Holy Spirit-inspired journey of how choices and agendas in the spirit realm have influenced and misdirected our path away from the perfect plan of God for His bride.

In order to find our way back into the incredible intimacy of relationship with God the Father, our Creator, it is essential to understand what went wrong.

Discover the truth about the subtleties of sin from the perspective of the Godhead.

Lucifer had it all but decided to take what belonged to everyone else.

The Lord says, "It's enough! It's time to take back what is rightfully the inheritance of the Body of Christ."

The Ancient Path is there to be discovered and enjoyed. And He wants you back on it towards Him, and the life, rewards and privilege He bought back for you on the cross.

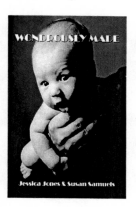

Wondrously Made is a look at the amazing co-relation of our human body and the city of Jerusalem. Since our creation came first, apparently we needed some further instruction on how we are to function. It lays out all the city gates, their meanings and functions and how they remarkably line up with our body gates. This book covers eight areas that need our attention in order to live a full, restored, abundant life in God.

The eleven gates of Jerusalem line up with the functions of our body, which lines up with the Christian walk from beginning to end. Learn to use the gates of Jerusalem in your Christian walk, move from born-again to full maturity. Understand the full inheritance waiting for you.